Che

First published in 2007 by Cherrytree Books,
a division of the Evans Publishing Group
2A Portman Mansions
Chiltern St
London W1U 6NR

Design. D.R.ink

British Library Cataloguing in Publication Data
Amos, Janine
      Cheat – (Good & Bad Series)
      I. Title II. Green, Gwen III. Series
      179.8

ISBN 1 842344 396 3
13 –digit ISBN (from 1 Jan 2007) 978 1 84234 396 8

Cheat

By Janine Amos

Illustrated by Gwen Green

CHERRYTREE BOOKS

Emma's story

"I can't do it!" said Emma, and she threw down her pen. Emma was at Becky's house after school. She was trying to write a poem.

"Mrs Lee said we all had to do one," said Becky. "Mine's about Thomas our cat."

"I think poems are silly," said Emma, crossly. But really she was worried. She couldn't think how to start.

"I've written lots of poems," said Becky's big sister Joanne.

"I'll show you, if you like. They might give you some ideas."

Joanne opened an exercise book. She passed it across to Emma and Becky. There was a poem called 'The Seaside'. There was one about Christmas. There was even a poem about a spider.

"I like the spider poem best," said Becky. Emma did, too.

Becky carried on writing her poem. Joanne started on her homework. But Emma sat staring at the spider poem. She read it again and again.

Emma looked at the empty paper in front of her. And still she couldn't think of anything to write. She felt a bit like crying.

Slowly, Emma started to copy out Joanne's poem. She did her best handwriting. She put her arms around the paper so the others couldn't see.

"Mrs Lee will be pleased," thought Emma, "and no one will ever know."

The next day at school, Mrs Lee asked everyone for their poems. Emma gave hers in last. Mrs Lee smiled at her, but Emma didn't smile back. She kept her head down and hurried back to her seat.

Mrs Lee looked at all the poems. She went over to Emma's desk.
"Did you write this all by yourself, Emma?" asked Mrs Lee.
Emma nodded but she didn't look up. She was too afraid.

Later Mrs Lee held up a big scrap book.

"I've put all your poems in this book," she said to the class.

"I'll pass it round for you to see. We'll start with Emma because her poem is at the front. It's all about a spider." And Mrs Lee put the book down on Emma's desk.

Suddenly, Becky jumped up from her seat.

"Let me see that spider poem," she said. She grabbed the book and read the words. She glared at Emma.

"That's my sister's poem!" said Becky loudly. "You cheat!" The whole class was listening. Emma went bright red.

How do you think Emma feels?

At break, Mrs Lee asked Emma to stay behind.

"Is it true that you didn't write the poem?" she asked.

Emma nodded.

"Can you tell me why?" asked Mrs Lee.

"I was scared," said Emma. "I couldn't think what to put."

"We all find things hard sometimes," said Mrs Lee. "But if that happens, you should talk to me about it. Cheating doesn't help anyone, does it?"

"No," agreed Emma, sadly.

How does Emma feel now?

After school, Becky wouldn't wait for Emma.

"Go away, Cheat!" said Becky, walking as fast as she could.

Emma had to run to catch up. "I'm sorry," said Emma. "Promise you won't tell Joanne?"

"All right," said Becky. "But I didn't like you cheating."

"Being a cheat was worse!" said Emma. And that made Becky laugh.

Feeling like Emma

Have you ever felt like Emma?
Have you ever cheated and been
found out? If you have, you'll
know how bad it feels. It makes
you ashamed.

Cheating

Emma pretended that someone
else's work was her own. Cheating
is about tricking other people. You
trick them into believing you've
done something when you haven't.

Cheating spoils things

Cheating can spoil things. It can spoil friendships. No one likes a cheat. And, as Emma's teacher said, cheating doesn't help anyone.

Asking for help

Emma's teacher understood about cheating. When Emma said she was afraid to write her own poem, Mrs Lee didn't mind. She said to ask for help next time. If you feel that you need to cheat, you could try talking about it first.

Peter's story

"Peep!" the whistle went – and they were off! Peter was in the lead. He came to the first hurdle – and cleared it in a huge leap. Peter could feel his heart thumping. His mouth was dry. The next hurdle was coming up.

It was School Sports Day. Peter was running in the hurdles race. There was a cup for the winner. And Peter wanted that cup.

Suddenly, Peter heard someone close behind him. Someone else was panting hard. Ben was catching him up!

The two boys ran on. They were well ahead of the others. Peter cleared the second hurdle, but he was slowing down. He turned his head – and there was Ben right alongside him.

"He's going to win!" thought Peter.

Just then, Peter pretended to wobble. He stuck out his arm – and he banged into Ben. Peter saw Ben stumble and fall on the grass. But Peter carried on running. He could see the finishing line just ahead.

After the race, Peter flopped down on the grass. He watched Ben come in second. Ben was dirty from his fall. His socks had slipped down. And he was crying.

Peter felt frightened. He wondered if anyone had seen him bump into Ben.

"Peter Brown!" went a loud voice. Peter jumped. His heart was beating fast again, as if he was still running.

"Peter Brown!" came the voice again. It was Mr Evans, the headmaster, calling Peter to come and collect his prize.

Peter went to the front and everyone clapped. Soon he was holding the cup in both hands.

Peter went to sit down. All the time, Ben was staring at him. Ben had black smears across his face, from the tears.

"You cheat!" he whispered as Peter went past. Peter pretended not to hear.

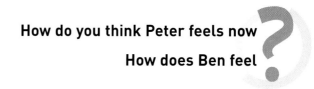

How do you think Peter feels now

How does Ben feel

At home, Peter went straight to his room. His big brother Tom was there, making a model plane. Peter threw the cup down on the bed.

"You won, then?" said Tom, looking at the cup.

"Not really," said Peter. "I cheated. I pushed Ben but nobody saw me. Have you ever cheated?" he asked his brother.

"Yes," said Tom. "And I've had people cheat me out of things, too. It's a horrible feeling."

"Shut up!" said Peter.

For a long time Peter sat and looked at the cup. He put it on his bookshelf. Then he took it down again. He knew he didn't want it any more. He gave a big sigh.

Tom looked up from his model. "Why don't you give the cup to Ben tomorrow?" he suggested. "That's what I'd do. It's better to be second than to be a cheat."

"I think you're right," said Peter at last.

Do you think Peter will give the cup to Ben

What would you do

Feeling like Peter

Peter wanted to win the cup. He wanted to win it so badly that he cheated to get it. But afterwards he didn't want the prize any more. Peter found out that a prize is only worth something if you've won it fairly.

Being cheated

Cheating isn't fair. Think how it feels to be cheated out of something, as Ben was. Thinking how someone else feels might stop you being a cheat in the future.

Kylie's story

Kylie's dad was working away from home. Kylie missed him a lot.

"I'll do him a drawing," she thought, "a special Welcome Home drawing."

Kylie was good at drawing and painting. And her dad was very proud of her. He always showed the drawings to his friends. "My daughter did that!" he told them. It made Kylie feel great.

Kylie found some paper and felt tips. She started a picture of a brown horse, but it didn't look right. Then she drew a fluffy grey cat. That was better but the tail was wrong. Kylie looked at her drawings.

"These aren't good enough. I want Dad to be really proud of me," she thought.

Kylie got out her new library book. She turned the pages until she found a picture of a rabbit. It was Kylie's favourite drawing in the whole book. The rabbit looked real.

"I wish I could draw like that," thought Kylie. "My dad would say I was brilliant."

Then Kylie had an idea.

What do you think Kylie will do

Carefully, Kylie put a piece of paper on top of the rabbit. She could just see the drawing underneath. Slowly, Kylie traced over the rabbit in the book.

"I'll tell Dad I thought up the drawing myself," Kylie said to herself. "I won't show him the book – and he'll never know."

Kylie coloured in the rabbit with her felt tips. She made it exactly the same colour as the library-book rabbit.

Later that day, Kylie's dad came home. His boss was with him and Kylie felt a bit shy. Kylie's dad gave her a hug. He looked at the drawing.

"This is wonderful!" said Kylie's dad. "You are clever!"

Kylie stared down at her feet. She didn't feel very happy.

Why doesn't Kylie feel happy

How do you think she feels

Kylie's dad held up the drawing. He showed it to his boss.

"Isn't my daughter a terrific artist?" asked Kylie's dad. He smiled at Kylie. "This is the best drawing you've ever done, Kylie," he said. "I'll get a frame for it. We'll put it on the wall!"

Kylie felt awful. She wished her dad would stop.

After supper, Kylie went to her room. She looked at the rabbit in her library book. And she snapped the book shut.

Kylie thought about her drawing. She felt a bit sick. She wished she'd done a different picture for her dad. She wished she'd done a drawing of her own.

Later, Kylie's mum came in. "You look sad!" she said to Kylie. "What's up?"

Kylie told her mum all about the drawing. She showed her the rabbit in the book.

"Dad's so pleased with me," said Kylie quietly. "I thought I'd feel great. But I don't. I hate that rabbit – and I hate myself!"

Why does Kylie hate herself?

Kylie's mum was quiet for a while. "You feel bad because you cheated," she said. "But you know that your dad's proud of what you do. There's no need to cheat."

Kylie didn't answer.

"Now what can you do tomorrow to make yourself feel better?" asked Kylie's mum.

"I could do a painting all on my own," said Kylie at last.

"Perhaps Dad will put it on the wall instead of the rabbit?"

"Perhaps he will," said Kylie's mum, smiling.

Feeling like Kylie

Kylie cheated because she thought it would please her father. He didn't catch her out – but she didn't feel happy about it. Whether you're found out or not, cheating doesn't feel good. Tricking people can make you feel uncomfortable. It can make you dislike yourself.

Talking about it

It's hard to own up to being a cheat. But it's often worse to keep the secret inside. If you've cheated and feel unhappy about it, try telling someone you trust. Talking about it might make you feel better. It might help you next time.

Why cheat?

Almost everyone feels like cheating sometimes. They cheat for different reasons. Sometimes they cheat because they feel they can't do something well enough. Or they might just be lazy, and cheating seems an easy way out. Sometimes people simply cheat to win.

Think about it

Think about the stories in this book. Emma, Peter and Kylie were all cheats. Do you feel like them sometimes? Next time you want to cheat, ask yourself some questions. What will I really gain by cheating? How will I feel afterwards? And what could I do instead?

If you are feeling frightened or unhappy, don't keep it to yourself. Talk to an adult you can trust, like a parent or a teacher. If you feel really alone, you could telephone or write to one of these offices. Remember, there is always someone who can help.

Childline
Freephone 0800 1111
Address: Freepost 1111, London N1 0BR
www.childline.org.uk

Childline for children in care
Freephone 0800 884444 (6 - 10pm)

NSPCC Child Protection Line
Freephone 0808 8005000
www.nspcc.org.uk

The Samaritans
08457 909090
www.samaritans.org.uk